Sheila Follows The Star

Illustrated by: Ella Tanner   Written by: Lynn Jupina

"For to us a child is born, to us a son is given; and the government will be on his shoulders. And he will be called Wonderful Counselor, Mighty God, Everlasting Father, Prince of Peace".

Isaiah 9:6

Sheila, the Not So Sheepish Sheep was a wanderer. She tried very hard to stay close-by to her shepherd, Mr. Sheraton Shepherd the Third. Sheila still remembers the last time she wandered off.

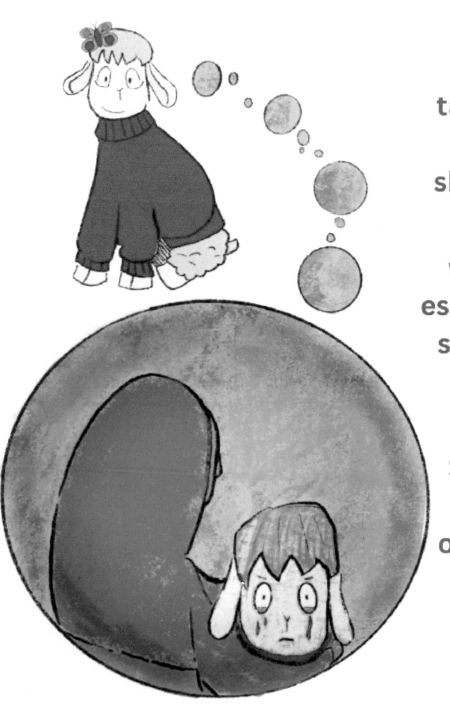

She got all tangled up in a bush during sheep shearing time and,

was so scared especially when it started raining.

BUT Mr. Sheraton Shepherd the Third left the other 99 sheep to find her.

Sometimes, though wanderlust, the need for adventure just got to her and she HAD to explore.

The good news is, she didn't wander very far from Mr. Sheraton Shepherd the Third, always keeping him in view and making sure she knew the way back to him.

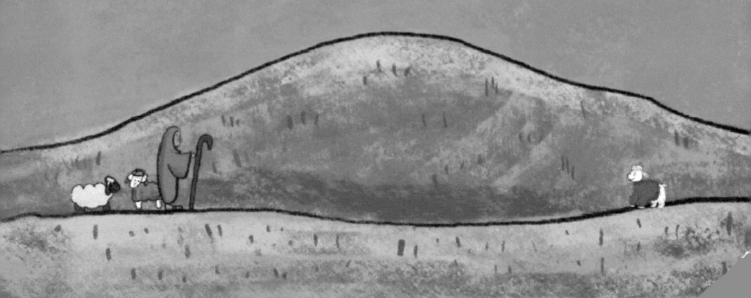

One night, after a busy day of wandering, when Sheila was safe and sound laying on her bed of hay, there was a bright star in the sky. The star looked like it was so close by she could touch it.

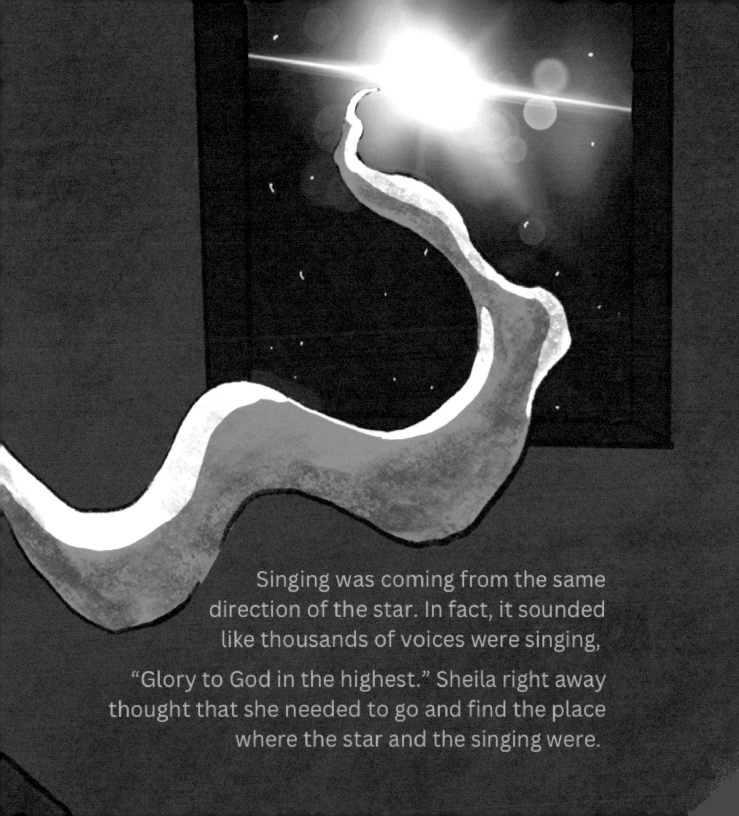

Singing was coming from the same direction of the star. In fact, it sounded like thousands of voices were singing,

"Glory to God in the highest." Sheila right away thought that she needed to go and find the place where the star and the singing were.

She had never EVER seen a star,
so big and bright and beautiful.
She just HAD to follow it.
BUT she didn't want Mr.
Sheraton Shepherd the Third
to worry about her.
BUT then again maybe she
would be back before he woke up.

BUT she also was a little fearful of going out at night by herself AND getting all tangled up in a bush again AND a little afraid of being far away from her Shepherd.

BUT that need for adventure took over, and she decided to leave Mr. Sheraton Shepherd the Third a note.

It read:

Dear Mr. Sheraton Shepherd the Third,

Please don't worry about me. I decided to follow the big, bright, beautiful star and the singing. I'll be back soon. I won't go far.

Love, Sheila

After having left the note, she went off skipping and laughing. Sheila was sure that she wouldn't be gone long. She followed the star and listened for the music. It was dark out, but she kept her eyes on the light.

All of the sudden, she heard footsteps behind her, and she got very frightened.

She remembered those BUT's always got her in trouble.

THUMP

She was afraid to turn around, so she began to walk faster. She could hear the footsteps going faster. SHE WAS SO SCARED! She started to shake.

When she finally turned around to see who or what was following her and she started laughing.

Why, it was her friends!

"Oh Sheila, slow down. I'm out of breath. Help me! you're killing me, slow down ."

Well, well, Sheila, I regret to tell you this, but you need to go a little slower here."

Shrill Sheldon the Showman was shouting.

Stanley, the Stern Sheriff bellowed.

Sobbing Socrates, followed
close behind, and was
sobbing loudly as he cried

Snappy Suzy, not to be
outdone, snapped

"Oh no, boo-hoo, boo-hoo,
where are we going? I am
so tired. Please, let's just
all go back to bed."

"Oh stop it, Socrates, just
keep walking. Did you hear
me? Just keep walking!
You're always fussing about
something!"

And then there was Snoring Sidney, you guessed it, he snored away, sleepwalking behind everyone." Behind them were 94 other sheep, followed by Mr. Sheraton Shepherd the Third.

Mr. Sheraton Shepherd the Third came running up to Sheila and said, "Oh Sheila there is no way we could ever let you do this journey alone. The star and the singing woke us up too, then I saw your note. We wanted to follow the star and singing too."

Sheila was so excited that all of her friends were going to follow the star with her. Best of all was the fact that Mr. Sheraton Shepherd the Third was there with them making sure they made it there safely.
As they walked along following the star, they laughed and talked about what they might find.

Shrill Sheldon, the Showman shouted, "Oh my! I'm sure it's something wonderful and exciting."

Stanley the Stern Sheriff bellowed, "Keep going, Sheldon! Why do you always have to be turning around to talk to everyone, You're going to cause a traffic jam! Move along!"

Sobbing Socrates sobbed the loudest he had EVER sobbed, "Oh what if it's not something wonderful! What if it's horrible and we all die? What if my feet hurt? What if it rains ...oh woe is me!"

Snappy Susan snapped, "Oh stop it, Socrates. Quit your crying Complain, complain ...shape up, Socrates!"

And of course, Snoring Sidney snored, sleepwalking never waking up the whole time."

After each step the star seemed brighter , and the singing seemed even louder and even more beautiful.
Sheila, the Not So Sheepish Sheep, knew whatever it was, it would be life changing. She just knew it in her heart.

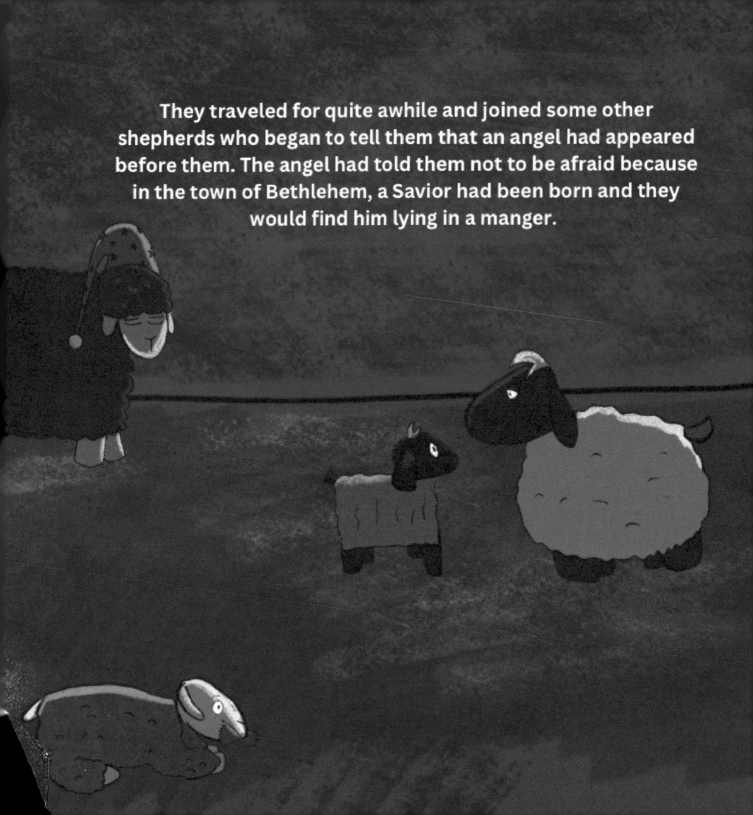

They traveled for quite awhile and joined some other shepherds who began to tell them that an angel had appeared before them. The angel had told them not to be afraid because in the town of Bethlehem, a Savior had been born and they would find him lying in a manger.

They also told them that a choir of angels had appeared and sang, " Glory to God in the highest! Peace and goodwill to everyone on earth!" They told Mr. Sheraton Shepherd, the Third, that they were also following the star. So they all rushed to Bethlehem where the angel had told them to go and they followed the star and the sound of the singing.

When they got to Bethlehem, there was a stable. Sheila the Not So Sheepish Sheep rushed past the other shepherds and all the other sheep. And there she met Jesus, the Savior of the world. He had come as a baby wrapped in swaddling clothes and lying in a manger just as promised. She was overcome with joy and filled with love and peace.

Sheila heard Shrill Sheldon the Showman, no longer shrill or showy, quietly whispering with awe in his voice, "Joy to the World, the Lord has come!"
Stanley the Stern Sheriff, no longer stern, gently said,
"This is the little Lord Jesus asleep in the hay."
Sobbing Socrates, no longer sobbing, could be heard through joyful tears,
"Let Heaven and earth rejoice!"

Snappy Susan no longer snapped at everyone but ever so gently said, "This, this is Christ the King."

And Snoring Sidney, you guessed it, he woke up and started jumping up and down singing, "Rejoice, rejoice the Lord has come."

Mr.Sheraton Shepherd the Third fell to his knees and worshipped Jesus.

Sheila, the Not So Sheepish Sheep, wanted to tell everyone all about Jesus who had come as a baby and would one day save the world from sin and sorrow and she did just that!!
As she and Mr. Sheridan Shepherd the Third traveled back to their pasture, they told everyone along the way about what they had seen and heard.
They had met the Savior of the world!